Guess Who
Jumps

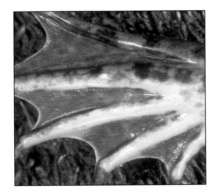

Dana Meachen Rau

Marshall Cavendish
Benchmark
New York

I live in a pond.

I sit on a log.

I have big eyes.

I look for flies to eat.

I eat worms, too.

I grab them with my sticky tongue.

My skin is wet.

I am green and brown.

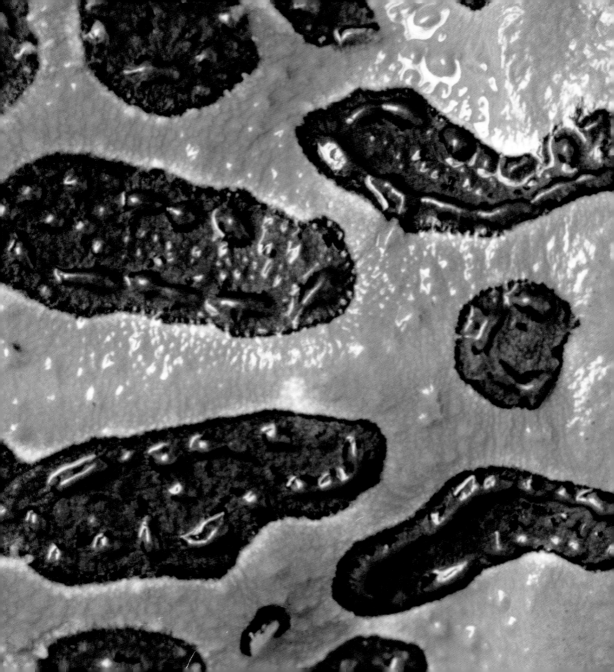

I can be loud.

My throat gets big when I *croak*.

My back legs are long.

My legs help me jump.

I lay eggs in the water.

My babies are *tadpoles*.

Tadpoles look like little fish.

They will grow legs.

They will lose their tails.

They will come out of the water.

The sun makes me hot.

I swim to cool off.

My back feet are *webbed*.

My back legs are strong.

I am a fast swimmer.

Who am I?

I am a frog!

Who am I?

eggs

eyes

legs

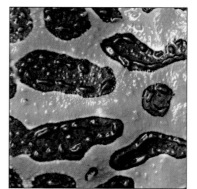

skin

28

tadpole

throat

Challenge Words

croak (krohk) The sound a frog makes.

tadpoles (TAD-pohls) Baby frogs that can live only in water.

webbed (webd) Having skin between the toes.

Index

Page numbers in **boldface** are illustrations.

About the Author

Dana Meachen Rau is the author of many other titles in the Bookworms series, as well as other nonfiction and early reader books. She lives in Burlington, Connecticut, with her husband and two children.

With thanks to the Reading Consultants:

Nanci Vargus, Ed.D., is an Assistant Professor of Elementary Education at the University of Indianapolis.

Beth Walker Gambro is an Adjunct Professor at the University of St. Francis in Joliet, Illinois.

Marshall Cavendish Benchmark
99 White Plains Road
Tarrytown, New York 10591-5502
www.marshallcavendish.us

Library of Congress Cataloging-in-Publication Data

Rau, Dana Meachen, 1971–
Guess who jumps / by Dana Meachen Rau.
p. cm. — (Bookworms. Guess who)
Summary: "Following a guessing game format, this book provides young readers with
clues about a frog's physical characteristics, behaviors, and habitats, challenging readers
to identify it"—Provided by publisher.
Includes index.
ISBN 978-0-7614-2908-1
1. Frogs—Juvenile literature. I. Title. II. Series.
QL668.E2R39 2009
597.8'9—dc22
2007024613

Editor: Christina Gardeski
Publisher: Michelle Bisson
Designer: Virginia Pope
Art Director: Anahid Hamparian

Photo Research by Anne Burns Images

Cover Photo by *Corbis*/Joe McDonald

The photographs in this book are used with permission and through the courtesy of:
Animals Animals: pp. 1, 23 Bill Beatty; pp. 17, 29L O.S.F.; p. 19 Scott W. Smith; p. 21 Stephen
Dalton/O.S.F. *Peter Arnold*: p. 3 PHONE/Thiriet Claudius; pp. 13, 28BL BIOS/Fischer Berndt;
p. 25 H.Frei. *Corbis*: pp. 5, 7, 11, 28TR, 29R Joe McDonald; pp. 9, 28BR Chris Mattison/Frank Lane
Picture Agency; pp. 15, 28TL Martin B. Withers/Frank Lane Picture Agency; p. 27 George McCarthy.

Printed in Malaysia
1 3 5 6 4 2